3
HA
D1035101

by Thomas Persano

Consultant: Marjorie Faulstich Orellana, PhD
Professor of Urban Schooling
University of California, Los Angeles

New York, New York

Credits

Cover, © Ronnachai Palas/Shutterstock and Sean Pavone/Shutterstock; TOC, © Du Zongjun/Dreamstime; 4, © Pius Lee/Shutterstock; 5T, © Jane Rix/Shutterstock; 5B, © kqlsm/Shutterstock; 7, © Sean Pavone/Shutterstock; 8, © martinho Smart/Shutterstock; 9, © tororo reaction/Shutterstock; 10, © Sorin Colac/Shutterstock; 11T, © PRILL/Shutterstock; 11B, © Phurinee Chinakathum/Shutterstock; 12T, Public Domain; 12B, © Bootzilla/iStock; 13, © Sean Pavone/Shutterstock; 14–15, © Sakarin Sawasdinaka/Shutterstock; 14L, © af8images/Shutterstock; 16, © aodaodaod/iStock; 17T, © jpskenn/iStock; 17B, © voyata/iStock; 18, © Devlin Anthony/PA Photos/ABACA/Newscom; 19, © Attila JANDI/Shutterstock; 20, © Sean Pavone/Shutterstock; 21, © Kyodo/Newscom; 22, © Boogich/iStock; 23, © TAGSTOCK1/iStock; 24T, © Bridgeman Images; 24B, © AF archive/Alamy Stock Photo; 25, © Stefano Politi Markovina/Alamy Stock Photo; 26L, © Baibaz/Dreamstime; 26–27, © danilovi/iStock; 28T, © J. Henning Buchholz/Shutterstock; 28B, © Mark Harwood/Alamy Stock Photo; 29, © Aflo Co. Ltd./Alamy Stock Photo; 30T, © Takeshi Nishio/Shutterstock, © ET1972/Shutterstock, and © Vladimir Wrangel/Shutterstock; 30B, © georgeclerk/iStock; 31 (T to B), © Fotos593/Shutterstock, Public Domain, © BlueOrange Studio/Shutterstock, © Devlin Anthony/PA Photos/ABACA/Newscom, and © voyata/Shutterstock; 32, © feiyuezhangjie/Shutterstock.

Publisher: Kenn Goin
Senior Editor: Joyce Tavolacci
Creative Director: Spencer Brinker
Design: Debrah Kaiser
Photo Researcher: Thomas Persano

Library of Congress Cataloging-in-Publication Data

Names: Persano, Thomas, author.
Title: Japan / by Thomas Persano.
Description: New York, New York : Bearport Publishing, 2018. | Series: Countries we come from | Audience: Ages 5 to 8. | Includes bibliographical references and index.
Identifiers: LCCN 2017007494 (print) | LCCN 2017010933 (ebook) | ISBN 9781684022533 (library) | ISBN 9781684023073 (ebook)
Subjects: LCSH: Japan—Juvenile literature.
Classification: LCC DS806 .P45 2018 (print) | LCC DS806 (ebook) | DDC 952—dc23
LC record available at https://lccn.loc.gov/2017007494

For more information, write to Bearport Publishing Company, Inc., 45 West 21st Street, Suite 3B, New York, New York 10010. Printed in the United States of America.

10 9 8 7 6 5 4 3 2 1

KAZAKHSTAN
MONGOLIA
CHINA
JAPAN
SAUDI
ARABIA
ETHIOPIA
TANZANIA
MOZAMBIQUE
MADAGASCAR
PHILIPPINES
Philippine Sea
PALAU
AUSTRALIA
Great Australian Bight
French Southern and Antarctic Lands

Contents

Bustling

和民
いだおれ
がんこ
道頓堀店
がんこ寿司
化粧品
道頓堀店
3F/4F
和民
大阪名物
欢迎光临
海鮮居酒屋
大阪名产物
大阪名物
CAFE
HERE ARE YOU

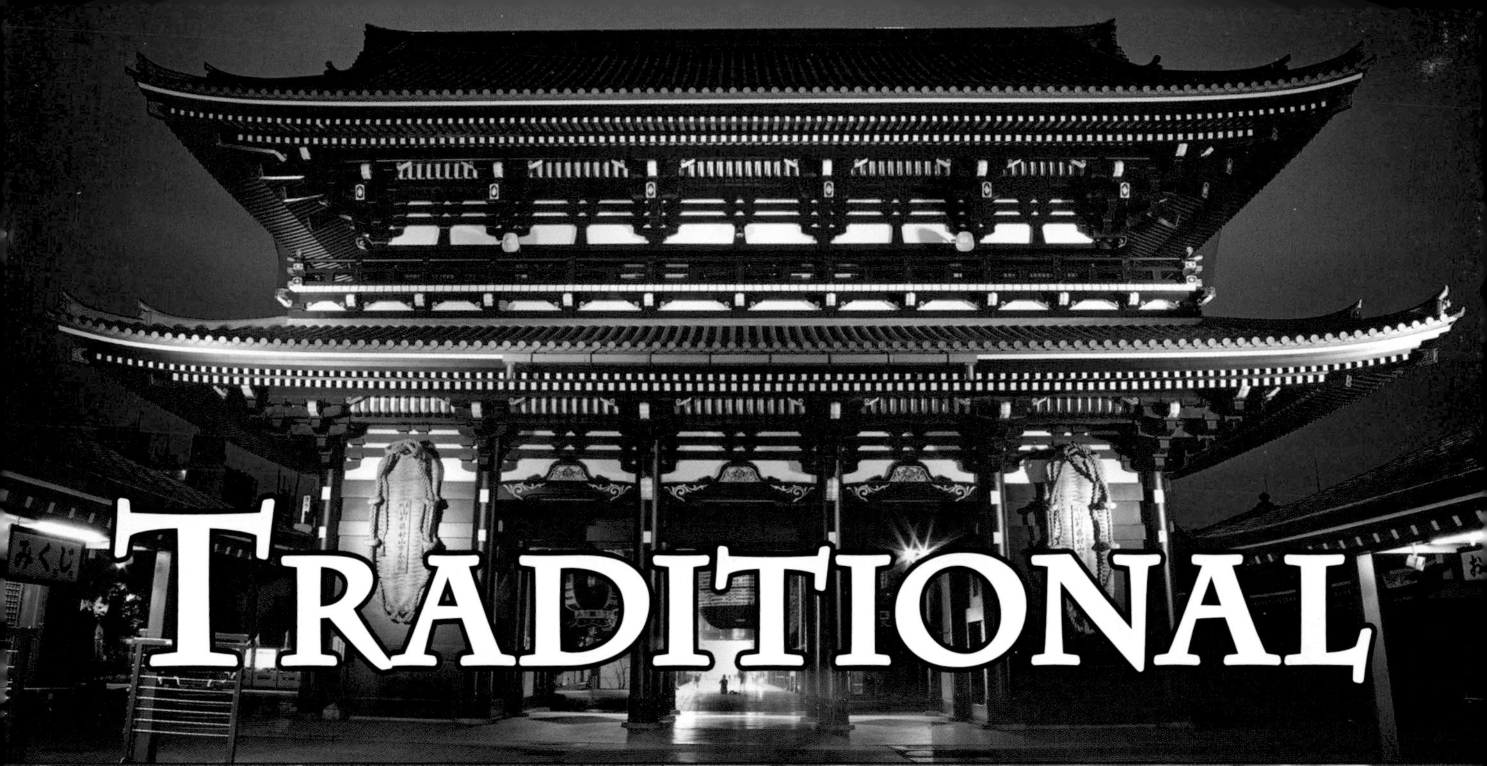

Traditional

Friendly

Welcome to Japan!

The country is made up of thousands of islands.

However, most people live on the four largest islands: Hokkaido, Honshu, Kyushu, and Shikoku.

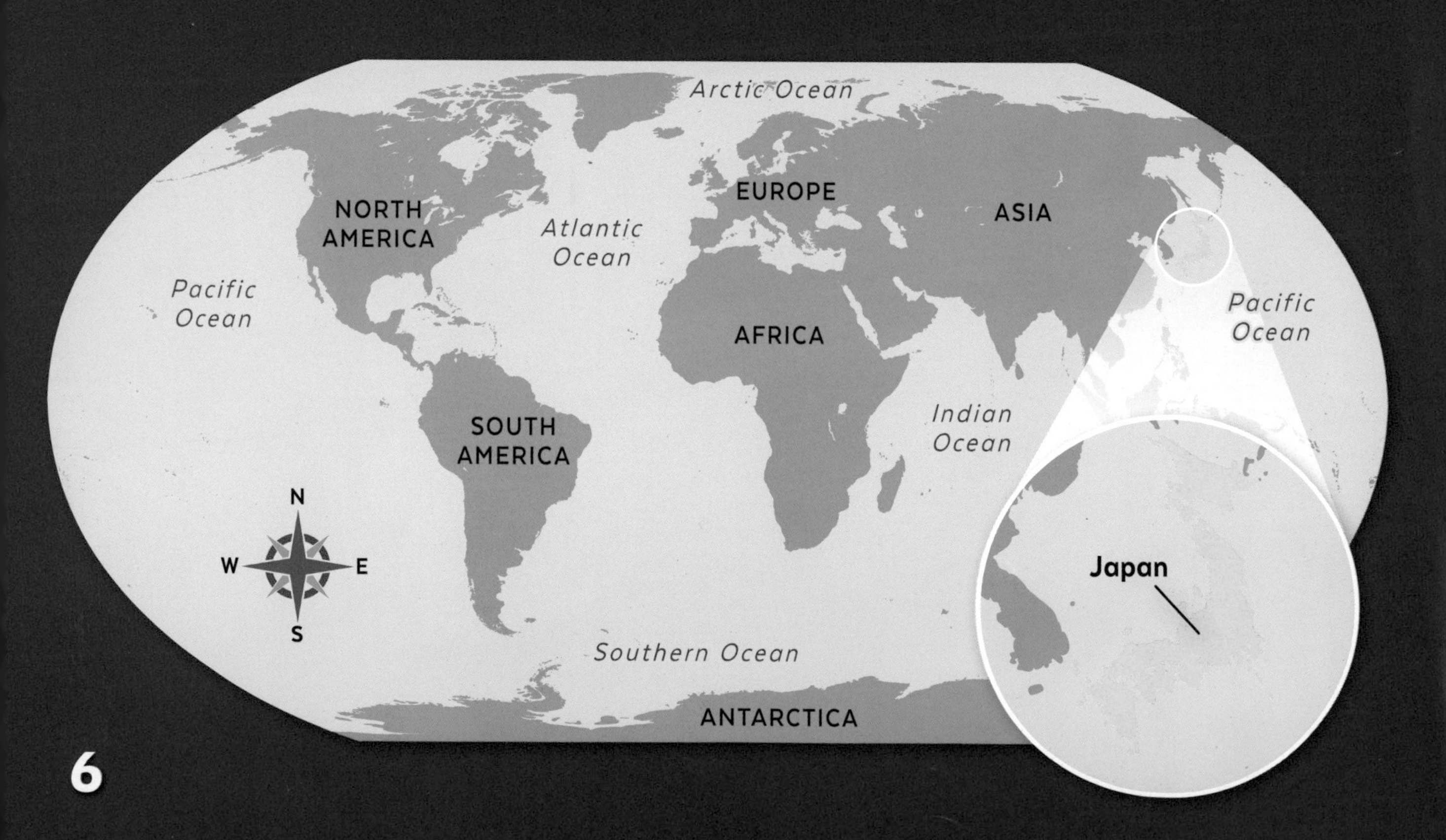

More than 127 million people call Japan home.

the city of Kobe on the island of Honshu

Mountains stretch across much of Japan.

Some are covered with snow.

Mount Fuji is Japan's highest mountain. It's also a **volcano**!

Areas near Japan's coast are warmer. Many of these places have sandy beaches.

the island of Okinawa

Macaque (*muh*-KAK) monkeys live in the snowy mountains.

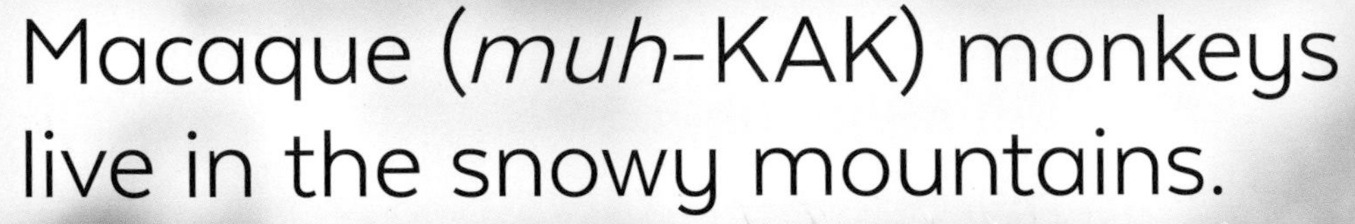

To keep warm, they soak in **hot springs**.

Tanukis are small raccoon-like animals.

They make their homes in Japan's thick forests.

Tanukis are a sign of good luck in Japan.

People have lived in Japan for thousands of years.

Long ago, powerful **emperors** and **shoguns** ruled the country.

They led fierce warriors called samurai in battles.

Shoguns built huge castles. Himeji Castle is one of the oldest. It dates to 1333.

Today, most people in Japan live in big cities.

Tokyo is the largest city in the country.

It's also Japan's **capital**.

People travel from city to city on high-speed trains called *Shinkansen*. The trains can go up to 200 miles per hour (322 kph)!

新宿駅東口
Shinjuku Sta. E. Ent.
Shinjukuogado nishi
新宿駅
300M

Many Japanese families live in traditional homes.

Thin mats called *tatami* cover the floor.

Sliding paper screens called *shoji* separate rooms.

Japan also has many modern buildings.

Japan is known for its **technology**.

Asimo is the name of a robot.

It can run, climb stairs, and even play soccer!

Some Japanese robots look and sound just like real people!

The Japanese have many festivals.

When the cherry trees bloom in spring, it's time for the Hanami festival.

People dine under the pink trees.

The *Aomori Nebuta* is a festival that takes place in summer. It's famous for its giant floats.

In Japan, people speak Japanese.

This is how you say *excuse me* in Japanese:

Sumimasen

(soo-mee-mah-sen)

This is how you say *see you later*:

Mata Ne

(mata nay)

Some Japanese words are borrowed from English. For example, *bakkupakku* means "backpack."

People of all ages read manga.

Manga are Japanese comic books.

In fact, there are cafés in Japan just for reading manga!

In Japan, more paper is used to print manga than to make toilet paper!

Yum! There's lots of tasty food in Japan.

The most famous dish is sushi.

It's made with raw fish and sticky rice.

A popular sport in Japan is sumo wrestling.

During a match, two huge men slam their bodies together.

The first man to push the other out of the ring wins!

Japanese people are also big fans of baseball.

Fast Facts

Capital city: Tokyo

Population of Japan: 127 million

Main language: Japanese

Money: Yen

Major religions: Shinto and Buddhism

Nearby countries include: China, North Korea, South Korea, and Russia

Cool Fact: There are more than 5.5 million vending machines in Japan. You can get drinks, books, and even eyeglasses from them!

Glossary

capital (KAP-uh-tuhl) a city where a country's government is based

emperors (EM-pur-urz) powerful rulers

hot springs (HOT SPRINGZ) water that's heated underground before flowing to the earth's surface

shoguns (SHOW-guhns) military rulers of Japan

technology (tek-NOL-uh-jee) the science of making useful things

volcano (vol-KAY-noh) a mountain that has an opening through which lava, rock, and gas can flow

Index

Read More

Moon, Walt K. *Let's Explore Japan (Let's Explore Countries).* Minneapolis, MN: Bumba Books (2017).

Sexton, Colleen. *Japan (Blastoff! Readers: Exploring Countries).* New York: Scholastic (2010).

Learn More Online

To learn more about Japan, visit
www.bearportpublishing.com/CountriesWeComeFrom

About the Author

Thomas Persano lived in Japan for two years. He spent his time exploring the country and eating lots of delicious Japanese food. He now lives in New York City with his wife, Molly.